A granny square CHRISTMAS™

What could be merrier than combining Christmas with the traditional granny square motif? Designer Lisa Gentry has put together a jolly collection of designs that will make decorating and gift-giving a treat for the maker and those who get to enjoy the results.

Decorate the tree and mantel with ornaments, a tree skirt, stocking and garland, then turn the couch into a cozy haven with the colorful blanket and pillow. There are even a mug cozy and trivet to brighten up the kitchen for Santa's visit. These treasures will quickly become a part of your family tradition. Lisa has also provided thoughtful gifts including a hat, scarf, cowl and fingerless mitts that will warm hearts as well as heads, necks and fingers. Make your family's Christmas extra-special with these timeless designs.

Bright & Happy Pillow, *page 24*

Winter Warmer
Mug Cozy, *page 27*
Trivet, *page 30*

Table of Contents

Decorate!

Cheerful Tree Skirt

Skill Level

 INTERMEDIATE

Finished Measurements

48 inches in diameter

Small Square: 3¼ inches across bottom x 2½ inches across top x 3¼ inches tall

Large Square: 10 inches across bottom x 6½ inches across top x 11 inches tall

Materials

- Medium (worsted) weight acrylic/wool yarn:
  10½ oz/600 yds/300g each red and off-white
  7 oz/400 yds/200g each green and lime green
- Size H/8/5mm crochet hook or size needed to obtain gauge
- Yarn needle

See page 45 for Yarn Specifics.

4 MEDIUM

Gauge

[Shell, ch 1] 4 times = 4 inches; 8 rnds = 4 inches

Pattern Notes

Skirt is worked in 3 sections: Outer Ring with Large Squares, Center Ring worked in rows along shorter side of Outer Ring, and then Inner Ring with Small Squares.

Squares are worked in joined rounds with right side facing at all times.

Weave in loose ends as work progresses.

Join with slip stitch as indicated unless otherwise stated.

Chain-3 at beginning of round counts as first double crochet unless otherwise stated.

Special Stitches

Beginning shell (beg shell): (Ch 3—*see Pattern Notes*, 2 dc) in indicated st or sp.

Shell: 3 dc in indicated st or sp.

Beginning 2-double crochet cluster (beg 2-dc cl): (Ch 3, dc) in indicated st or sp.

Corner shell: (3 dc, ch 2, 3 dc) in indicated st or sp.

2-double crochet cluster (2-dc cl): Yo, insert hook in indicated st or sp, yo, draw up a lp, yo and draw through 2 lps on hook *(2 lps on hook)*, yo, insert hook in indicated st or sp, yo, draw up a lp, yo, draw through 2 lps on hook, yo, draw through all 3 lps on hook.

Cluster decrease (cl dec): Dc in indicated sp, work 2-dc cl in same sp and in next indicated sp, dc in same sp as last sp.

3-double crochet cluster (3-dc cl): Yo, insert hook in indicated st or sp, yo, draw up a lp, yo, draw through 2 lps on hook *(2 lps on hook)*, [yo, insert hook in same st, yo, draw up a lp, yo, draw through 2 lps on hook] twice, yo, draw through all 4 lps on hook.

Color Sequence

Large Square

Note: *Change color each rnd as follows.*

Squares 1, 5, 9 & 13: [Off-white, dark green, lime green and red] twice, off-white and dark green.

Squares 2, 6, 10 & 14: [Red, off-white, dark green and lime green] twice, red and off-white.

Squares 3, 7 & 11: [Dark green, lime green, red and off-white] twice, dark green and lime green.

Squares 4, 8 & 12: [Lime green, red, off-white and dark green] twice, lime green and red.

Small Square

Note: *Work rnds 1 and 2 with first color listed, then rnd 3 with 2nd color listed as follows:*

Squares 1 & 10: Off-white, dark green.

Square 2: Lime green, red.

Square 3: Dark green, off-white.

Squares 4 & 7: Off-white, red.

Square 5: Red, dark green.

Square 6: Lime green, off-white.

Square 8: Dark green, lime green.

Squares 9 & 12: Red, off-white.

Square 11: Dark green, red.

Tree Skirt

Outer Ring

Large Square
Make 14 referring to Color Sequence.

Rnd 1 (RS): With first color, ch 4, **join** *(see Pattern Notes)* in first ch to form a ring, **beg shell** *(see Special Stitches)* in ring, ch 2, (**shell**—*see Special Stitches*, ch 2) 3 times in ring, join in 3rd ch of beg ch-3. Fasten off. *(4 shells, 4 ch-2 sps)*

Rnd 2: Join next color in next ch-2 corner sp, (**beg 2-dc cl**—*see Special Stitches*, ch 2, shell, ch 1) in same ch-2 sp, [**corner shell** *(see Special Stitches)*, ch 1] in each of next 2 ch-2 sps, (shell, ch 2, **2-dc cl** *(see Special Stitches)*, ch 1) in next ch-2 sp, join in beg cl. Fasten off. *(6 shells, 2 2-dc cls, 4 ch-2 sps, 4 ch-1 sps)*

Rnd 3: Join next color in next ch-2 corner sp, (beg 2-dc cl, ch 2, shell, ch 1) in same ch-2 sp as join, shell, ch 1 in next ch-1 sp, *corner shell, ch 1 in next corner shell, shell, ch 1 in next ch-1 sp, rep from *, (shell, ch 2, 2-dc cl, ch 1) in next ch-2 sp, 2-dc cl, ch 1 in next ch-1 sp, join in beg cl. Fasten off. *(9 shells, 3 2-dc cls, 4 ch-2 sps, 8 ch-1 sps)*

Rnd 4: Join next color in next ch-2 corner sp, (beg 2-dc cl, ch 2, shell, ch 1) in same ch-2 sp as join, [shell, ch 1] in each ch-1 sp to next ch-2 corner, *corner shell, ch 1 in next corner shell, [shell, ch 1] in each ch-1 sp to next ch-2 corner, rep from *, (shell, ch 2, 2-dc cl, ch 1) in next ch-2 space, 2-dc cl, ch 1 in each ch-1 sp to next cluster, join to beg cl. Fasten off. *(12 shells, 4 2-dc cls, 4 ch-2 sps, 12 ch-1 sps)*

Rnds 5–8: Rep rnd 4. *(24 shells, 8 2-dc cls, 4 ch-2 sps, 24 ch-1 sps)*

Rnd 9: Join next color in next ch-2 corner sp, (beg shell, ch 2, shell, ch 1) in same ch-2 sp as join, *[shell, ch 1] in each ch-1 sp to next ch-2 corner, corner shell, ch 1 in next corner shell, rep from * twice, [2-dc cl, ch 1] in each ch-1 sp to next corner shell, join in 3rd ch of beg ch-3. Fasten off. *(29 shells, 7 2-dc cls, 4 ch-2 sps, 28 ch-1 sps)*

Rnd 10: Rep rnd 9. Fasten off. *(32 shells, 8 2-dc cls, 4 ch-2 sps, 32 ch-1 sps)*

Assembly
Arrange Large Squares for Outer Ring referring to Placement Diagram, with RS facing, **whipstitch** *(see illustration)* Squares tog.

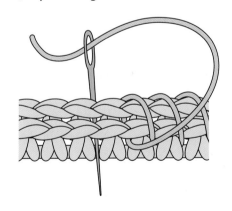

Whipstitch Edges

Center Ring
Row 1 (RS): Holding Outer Ring with RS facing and working across shorter inner edge, join off-white in first ch-2 corner sp, (beg shell, ch 1) in same ch-2 sp as join, *[shell, ch 1 in next ch-1 sp, sk next ch-1 sp] 4 times, shell, ch 1 in next ch-1 sp**, **cl dec** *(see Special*

Stitches) in next 2 ch-2 corner sps, ch 1, rep from * 13 times, ending last rep at **, shell in last ch-2 corner sp. Fasten off. *(85 shells, 84 ch-1 sps)*

Row 2 (RS): Join dark green in first dc of previous row, ch 4, (shell, ch 1) in each ch-1 sp across row, dc in last dc. Fasten off. *(84 shells, 2 dc, 85 ch-1 sps)*

Row 3 (RS): Join off-white in first dc of previous row, (beg shell, ch 1) in same dc as join, [shell, ch 1] in each of next 16 ch-1 sps, *work cl dec in next 2 ch-1 sps, ch 1, (shell, ch 1) in each of next 10 ch-1 sps, rep from * 4 times, (shell, ch 1) in each rem ch-1 sp across, shell in last dc. Fasten off. *(80 shells, 79 ch-1 sps)*

Row 4 (RS): With red, rep row 2. *(79 shells, 2 dc, 80 ch-1 sps)*

Row 5 (RS): Join off-white in first dc of previous row, (beg shell, ch 1) in same dc as join, (shell, ch 1) in each of next 3 ch-1 sps, *work cl dec in next 2 ch-1 sps, ch 1, (shell, ch 1) in each of next 8 ch-1 sps, rep from * 7 times, work cl dec in next 2 ch-1 sps, ch 1, (shell, ch 1) in each of next 2 ch-1 sps, shell in last dc. Fasten off. *(72 shells, 71 ch-1 sps)*

Row 6 (RS): With red, rep row 2. *(71 shells, 2 dc, 72 ch-1 sps)*

Row 7 (RS): Join off-white in first dc of previous row, (beg shell, ch 1) in same dc as join, (shell, ch 1) in each of next 2 ch-1 sps, *work cl dec in next 2 ch-1 sps, ch 1**, (shell, ch 1) in each of next 7 ch-1 sps, rep from * 7 times, work cl dec in next 2 ch-1 sps, ch 1, (shell, ch 1) in each of next 4 ch-1 sps, shell in last dc. Fasten off. *(64 shells, 63 ch-1 sps)*

Row 8 (RS): With lime green, rep row 2. *(63 shells, 2 dc, 64 ch-1 sps)*

Row 9: Join off-white in first dc of previous row, (beg shell, ch 1) in same dc as join, (shell, ch 1) in each of next 5 ch-1 sps, *work cl dec in next 2 ch-1 sps, ch 1, (shell, ch 1) in each of next 6 ch-1 sps, rep from * 6 times, work cl dec in next 2 ch-1 sps, ch 1, (shell, ch 1) in next ch-1 sp, shell in last dc. Fasten off. *(57 shells, 56 ch-1 sps)*

Row 10 (RS): With red, rep row 2. *(56 shells, 2 dc, 57 ch-1 sps)*

Row 11 (RS): Join off-white in first dc of previous row, (beg shell, ch 1) in same dc as join, (shell, ch 1) in each of next 4 ch-1 sps, *work cl dec in next 2 ch-1 sps, ch 1, (shell, ch 1) in each of next 7 ch-1 sps, rep from * 4 times, work cl dec in next 2 ch-1 sps, ch 1, (shell, ch 1) in each of next 5 ch-1 sps, shell in last dc. Fasten off. *(51 shells, 50 ch-1 sps)*

Row 12 (RS): With red, rep row 2. *(50 shells, 2 dc, 51 ch-1 sps)*

Row 13 (RS): Join off-white in first dc of previous row, (beg shell, ch 1) in same dc as join, (shell, ch 1) in each of next 7 ch-1 sps, *work cl dec in next 2 ch-1 sps, ch 1, (shell, ch 1) in each of next 9 ch-1 sps, rep from * twice, work cl dec in next 2 ch-1 sps, ch 1, (shell, ch 1) in each of next 7 ch-1 sps, shell in last dc. Fasten off. *(47 shells, 46 ch-1 sps)*

Row 14: With dark green, rep row 2. *(46 shells, 2 dc, 47 ch-1 sps)*

Row 15: Join off-white in first dc of previous row, (beg shell, ch 1) in same dc as join, (shell, ch 1) in each of next 2 ch-1 sps, *3-dc cl *(see Special Stitches)* in next ch-1 sp, ch 1, (shell, ch 1) in each of next 3 ch-1 sps, rep from * 10 times, 3-dc cl in next ch-1 sp, ch 1, (shell, ch 1) in each of next 2 ch-1 sps, shell in last dc. Fasten off. *(36 shells, 11 3-dc cls, 46 ch-1 sps)*

Inner Ring

Small Square
Make 12 referring to Color Sequence.

Rnd 1 (RS): With first color, ch 4, join in first ch to form a ring, beg shell in ring, ch 2, [shell in ring, ch 2] 3 times, join in 3rd ch of beg ch-3. *(4 shells, 4 ch-2 sps)*

Rnd 2: Sl st in next 2 dc, sl st in ch-2 sp, (beg 2-dc cl, ch 2, shell, ch 1) in same ch-2 sp as join, [corner shell, ch 1] in each of next 2 ch-2 sps, (shell, ch 2, 2-dc cl, ch 1) in next ch-2 sp, join in first cl. Fasten off. *(6 shells, 2 2-dc cls, 4 ch-2 sps, 4 ch-1 sps)*

Rnd 3: Join next color in next ch-2 corner sp, (beg 2-dc cl, ch 2, shell, ch 1) in same ch-2 sp as join, (shell, ch 1) in next ch-1 sp, *(corner shell, ch 1) in next corner shell, (shell, ch 1) in next ch-1 sp, rep from *, (shell, ch 2, 2-dc cl, ch 1) in next ch-2 sp, (2-dc cl, ch 1) in next ch-1 sp, join in first cl. Fasten off. *(9 shells, 3 2-dc cls, 4 ch-2 sps, 8 ch-1 sps)*

Assembly
Arrange Small Squares for Inner Ring referring to Placement Diagram. With RS facing, whipstitch the Small Squares tog.

With finished Inner Ring and Center Ring RS facing, whipstitch longer edge from Inner Ring to Center ring.

Edging
Rnd 1 (RS): Join red in Inner Ring corner to work across inner edge, ch 1, work sc in each st across inner edge, work 3 sc in next corner, work sc evenly across side opening to next corner, work 3 sc in corner, at outer edge work 1 sc in each dc and ch-1 sp and 2 sc in each ch-2 corner sp across the 14 squares, work 3 sc in next corner, work sc evenly across other side opening, join to beg sc. Fasten off. ●

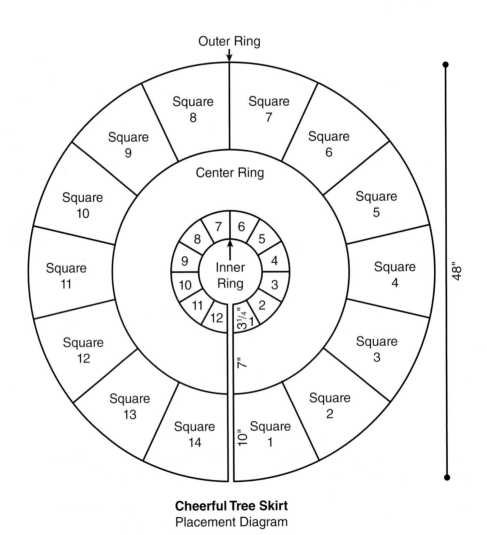

Cheerful Tree Skirt
Placement Diagram

Decorate!

Merry Stocking

Skill Level
■■■□ INTERMEDIATE

Finished Measurements
5½ inches wide across Leg x 17 inches long

Materials

- Medium (worsted) weight acrylic/wool yarn:
    3½ oz/200 yds/100g each red-and-green variegated, red, off-white and dark green
- Size H/8/5mm crochet hook or size needed to obtain gauge
- Yarn needle

See page 45 for Yarn Specifics.

Gauge
[Shell, ch 1] 4 times = 3½ inches; 3 Stocking rnds = 1¾ inches

Pattern Notes
Weave in loose ends as work progresses.

Join with slip stitch as indicated unless otherwise stated.

Chain-3 at beginning of round counts as first double crochet unless otherwise stated.

Special Stitches
Beginning shell (beg shell): (Ch 3, 2 dc) in indicated st or sp.

Shell: 3 dc in indicated st or sp.

Corner shell: (3 dc, ch 2, 3 dc) in indicated st or sp.

Color Sequence
Change color each rnd of each Square as follows:

Square 1: Dark green, off-white and red.

Square 2: Dark green, red and off-white.

Square 3: Off-white, dark green and red.

Square 4: Red, dark green and off-white.

Stocking

Leg
Rnd 1 (RS): Beg at top of Stocking with variegated, ch 48, **join** *(see Pattern Notes)* in first ch to form a ring, ch 1, sc in each ch around, join in beg sc. *(48 sc)*

Rnd 2: Ch 3 *(see Pattern Notes)*, dc in each of next 2 sc, ch 1, sk next sc, [dc in each of next 3 sc, ch 1, sk next sc] 11 times, join in 3rd ch of beg ch-3. *(12 shells, 12 ch-1 sps)*

Rnd 3: Sl st in next 2 dc, sl st in next ch-1 sp, **beg shell** *(see Special Stitches)* in same ch-1 sp, [**shell** *(see Special Stitches)* in next ch-1 sp, ch 1] around, join in 3rd ch of beg ch-3. *(12 shells)*

Rnds 4–20: Rep rnd 3. At the end of rnd 20, fasten off.

Heel
Row 1: Join red in first dc of shell, ch 1, sc in each of next 3 dc, [sk next ch-1 sp, sc in each of next 3 dc] 6 times, turn. *(21 sc)*

Row 2: Ch 1, sc in each of next 14 sc, leaving rem sts unworked, turn. *(14 sc)*

Row 3: Ch 1, sc in each of next 7 sc, leaving rem sts unworked, turn. *(7 sc)*

ch 1] 5 times, *sk next sc of Heel, dc in each of next 3 sc of Heel, ch 1, rep from * 4 times, join in 3rd ch of beg ch-3. *(11 shells)*

Rnd 2: Sl st in each of next 2 dc, sl st in next ch-1 sp, beg shell in same ch-1 sp, ch 1, [shell in next ch-1 sp, ch 1] around, join in 3rd ch of beg ch-3. *(11 shells)*

Rnds 3–10: Rep rnd 2. At the end of rnd 10, fasten off.

Toe

Rnd 1: Join red in first dc of any shell, ch 1, sc in same dc as beg ch-1, sc in each of next 2 dc, sk next ch-1 sp, [sc in each of next 3 dc, sk next ch-1 sp] around, join in beg sc. *(33 sc)*

Rnd 2: Ch 1, [sc in each of next 9 sc, **sc dec** *(see Stitch Guide)* in next 2 sc] 3 times, join in beg sc. *(30 sc)*

Rnd 3: Ch 1, [sc in each of next 4 sc, sc dec in next 2 sc] 5 times, join in beg sc. *(25 sc)*

Rnd 4: Ch 1, [sc in each of next 3 sc, sc dec in next 2 sc] 5 times, join in beg sc. *(20 sc)*

Rnd 5: Ch 1, [sc in each of next 3 sc, sc dec in next 2 sc] 4 times, join in beg sc. *(16 sc)*

Rnd 6: Ch 1, [sc in each of next 2 sc, sc dec in next 2 sc] 4 times, join in beg sc. *(12 sc)*

Rnd 7: Ch 1, [sc dec in next 2 sc] 6 times, join in beg sc, leaving 12-inch length of yarn, fasten off. *(6 sc)*

Cuff

Square
Make 4 referring to Color Sequence.

Rnd 1 (RS): With first color, ch 4, join to form a ring, beg shell in ring, ch 2, (shell in ring, ch 2) 3 times, join in 3rd ch of beg ch-3. Fasten off. *(4 shells, 4 ch-2 sps)*

Rnd 2 (RS): Join next color in any ch-2 sp, (beg shell, ch 2, shell) in same ch-2 sp, ch 1, [**corner shell** *(see Special Stitches)* in next ch-2 sp, ch 1] 3 times, join in 3rd ch of beg ch-3. Fasten off. *(8 shells, 4 ch-2 sps, 4 ch-1 sps)*

Row 4: Ch 1, sc in each of next 7 sc, sc in next unworked st of row 1 of Heel, turn. *(8 sc)*

Row 5: Ch 1, sc in each of next 8 sc, sc in next unworked sc of row 2 of Heel, turn. *(9 sc)*

Row 6: Ch 1, sc in each sc across previous row, sc in next unworked sc of row 1 of Heel, turn. *(10 sc)*

Rep rows 5 and 6 until all Heel sts of rows 1 and 2 are worked. Fasten off. *(21 sc)*

Foot
Rnd 1 (RS): Join variegated in first ch-1 sp after Heel, beg shell in same ch-1 sp, ch 1, [shell in next ch-1 sp,

Rnd 3: Join next color in any ch-2 corner sp, (beg shell, ch 2, shell) in same ch-2 sp, ch 1, shell in next ch-1 sp, ch 1, [corner shell in next ch-2 sp, ch 1, shell in next ch-1 sp, ch 1] 3 times, join in 3rd ch of beg ch-3. Fasten off. *(12 shells, 4 ch-2 sps, 8 ch-1 sps)*

Thread yarn needle with length of yarn, **whipstitch edges** *(see illustration)* of Squares tog into a 4-Square strip. Whipstitch ends of first and 4th Squares tog to form a circle.

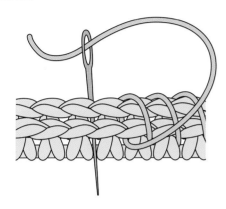

Whipstitch Edges

Top Trim

Rnd 1 (RS): Align seam between Squares 1 and 4 with center back of Leg in line with Heel, holding WS of Cuff tog with RS of Leg and working through both thicknesses, join variegated in top edge of Cuff seam, ch 1, work 12 sc across each Square, join in beg sc. Fasten off. *(48 sc)*

Rnd 2: Join off-white with sl st in first sc of rnd 1, ch 3, sl st in 2nd ch from hook, sk next sc, [sl st in next sc, ch 3, sl st in 2nd ch from hook, sk next sc] around, join in beg sl st, ch 15 *(for hanging lp)*, sl st in beg sl st. Fasten off.

Bottom Trim

Rnd 1 (RS): Join variegated at side seam, ch 1, work 12 sc across each Square, join in beg sc. Fasten off. *(48 sc)*

Rnd 2: Join off-white with sl st in first sc of rnd 1, ch 3, sl st in 2nd ch from hook, sk next sc, [sl st in next sc, ch 3, sl st in 2nd ch from hook, sk next sc] around, join in beg sl st. Fasten off. ●

Garland

Skill Level

 EASY

Finished Measurements

46 inches wide, excluding hanging loops x 4¾ inches long

Materials

- Medium (worsted) weight acrylic/wool yarn:
  3½ oz/200 yds/100g each red-and-green variegated, red, off-white, dark green, bright orange, pale blue, lime green, pale green and pale pink
- Size H/8/5mm crochet hook or size needed to obtain gauge
- Yarn needle
- 1-inch multicolored ornaments: 7

See page 45 for Yarn Specifics.

Gauge

Triangle = 4¾ inches long

Pattern Notes

Weave in loose ends as work progresses.

Join with slip stitch as indicated unless otherwise stated.

Chain-3 at beginning of round counts as first double crochet unless otherwise stated.

Special Stitches

Beginning shell (beg shell): (**Ch 3**—*see Pattern Notes*, 2 dc) in indicated st or sp.

Shell: 3 dc in indicated st or sp.

Corner shell: (3 dc, ch 3, 3 dc) in indicated st or sp.

Picot: Ch 3, sl st in 3rd ch from hook.

Color Sequence

Triangles 1 & 5: Work 1 rnd each variegated, off-white, red and dark green.

Triangles 2 & 6: Work 1 rnd each pale blue, red, lime green and dark green.

Triangles 3 & 7: Work 1 rnd each bright orange, pale green, red and dark green.

Triangles 4 & 8: Work 1 rnd each off-white, red, pale pink and dark green.

Garland

Triangle Motif

Make 8 referring to Color Sequence.

Rnd 1 (RS): With first color, ch 4, **join** *(see Pattern Notes)* in first ch to form a ring, **beg shell** *(see Special Stitches)* in ring, ch 3, (**shell**—*see Special Stitches,*

ch 3) twice in ring, join in 3rd ch of beg ch-3. Fasten off. *(3 shells, 3 ch-2 sps)*

Rnd 2: Join next color in any ch-3 sp, (beg shell, ch 3, shell) in same ch-3 sp, ch 2, [**corner shell** *(see Special Stitches)* in next ch-3 sp, ch 2] twice, join in 3rd ch of beg ch-3. Fasten off. *(3 corner shells, 3 ch-2 sps)*

Rnd 3: Join next color in any ch-3 corner sp, (beg shell, ch 3, shell) in same ch-3 sp, ch 2, shell in next ch-2 sp, ch 2, [corner shell in next ch-3 sp, ch 2, shell in next ch-2 sp, ch 2] twice, join in 3rd ch of beg ch-3. Fasten off. *(3 corner shells, 3 shells, 6 ch-2 sps)*

Rnd 4: Join next color in any ch-3 sp, (beg shell, ch 3, shell) in same ch-3 sp, ch 1, [shell in next ch-2 sp, ch 2] across to next corner ch-3, corner shell in next ch-3 sp, **picot** *(see Special Stitches)*, [shell in next ch-2 sp, picot] twice, (shell, picot, shell) in next corner ch-3 sp, [picot, shell in next ch-2 sp] twice, picot, join in 3rd ch of beg ch-3. Fasten off. *(3 corner shells, 6 shells, 9 ch-2 sps, 7 picots)*

Arrange Triangles in numerical order with picot corner shell pointing downward.

Garland String

Row 1 (RS): With off-white, ch 11, join in first ch *(for hanging lp)*, ch 15, with RS facing, pick up first Triangle Motif, *work 2 sc in right corner ch-3 sp, sc in each

st across straight edge to next corner ch-3 sp, 2 sc in corner ch-3 sp**, ch 4, pick up next Triangle Motif, rep from * across, ending last rep at **, ch 26, sl st in 11th ch from hook *(for hanging lp)*. Fasten off.

Attaching Ornaments

Cut 10-inch length of red, fold in half, insert hook into hanger of ornament, draw through to form a lp, draw cut ends through lp on hook. Holding both ends tog, insert hook in ch-4 sp of Garland String between Triangle Motifs and draw ends through, knot ends to secure from passing through ch, tie ends in a bow. To keep plies from unraveling, knot end of each rem strand. Rep until all ornaments are attached in ch-4 sp between Triangle Motifs. ●

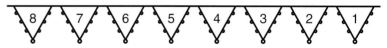

Garland
Placement Diagram

Keepsake Ornaments

Skill Level

 EASY

Finished Measurements

Stocking: 2½ inches wide x 4¼ inches long

Tree: 4 inches wide at widest point x 4½ inches long, including Tree Trunk

Star: 5 inches in diameter

Materials

- Medium (worsted) weight acrylic/wool yarn:
  25 yds each dark green, red, lime green and off-white
- Size H/8/5mm crochet hook or size needed to obtain gauge
- Yarn needle

See page 45 for Yarn Specifics.

Gauge

Stocking: Rnds 1–3 = 4¾ inches in diameter; rnds 1 and 2 = 2½ inches square

Pattern Notes

Materials listed will make 1 of each ornament.

Weave in loose ends as work progresses.

Join with slip stitch as indicated unless otherwise stated.

Chain-6 at beginning of round counts as first double crochet and chain-3 unless otherwise stated.

Chain-3 at beginning of round counts as first double crochet unless otherwise stated.

Special Stitches

Shell: 3 dc in indicated st or sp.

Beginning shell (beg shell): (Ch 3, 2 dc) in indicated st or sp.

Corner shell: (3 dc, ch 2, 3 dc) in indicated st or sp.

Stocking

Rnd 1 (RS): With red, ch 4, **join** *(see Pattern Notes)* in first ch to form a ring, **beg shell** *(see Special Stitches)* in ring, ch 2, (**shell**—*see Special Stitches* in ring, ch 2) 3 times in ring, join in 3rd ch of beg ch-3. Fasten off. *(4 shells, 4 ch-2 sps)*

Note: *If desired, work solid-color Stocking by omitting color changes.*

Rnd 2: Join lime green in any ch-2 sp, (beg shell, ch 2, shell, ch 1) in same ch-2 sp, (**corner shell**—*see Special Stitches*, ch 1) in each of next 3 ch-2 sps, join in 3rd ch of beg ch-3. Fasten off. *(8 shells, 4 ch-2 sps, 4 ch-1 sps)*

Rnd 3: Join off-white in any ch-2 corner sp, (beg shell, ch 2, shell, ch 1) in same ch-2 sp, (shell, ch 1) in next ch-1 sp, (corner shell, ch 1) in next corner shell, (shell, ch 1) in next ch-1 sp, (shell, ch 2, 3 tr) in next corner shell, tr in each of next 3 sts, (3 tr, 2 **dtr**—*see Stitch*

Guide, 3 tr) in next ch-1 sp, tr in each of next 3 sts, (3 tr, ch 2, shell, ch 1) in next corner shell, shell in next ch-1 sp, ch 1, join in 3rd ch of beg ch-3. Fasten off. *(2 corner shells, 15 dc, 18 tr, 2 dtr)*

Edging

Join red in next ch-2 corner sp, sc in same sp and in next 11 sts, fold piece in half with WS tog to form a boot, working through both thicknesses, (sc, ch 15, sl st in 15th ch from hook, sc) in corner ch-2 sp for hanging lp, sc in each of next 11 sts, (sc, ch 1, sc) in corner ch-2 sp, sc in each of next 10 sts. Fasten off.

Tree

Rnd 1 (RS): With dark green, ch 4, **join** *(see Pattern Notes)* in first ch to form a ring, **ch 6** *(see Pattern Notes)*, (**shell**—*see Special Stitches*, ch 3) twice in ring, 2 dc in ring, join in 3rd ch of beg ch-6. *(3 shells, 3 ch-3 sps)*

Rnd 2: Sl st in center of ch-3 sp, (**ch 3**—*see Pattern Notes*, 2 dc, ch 2) in same sp, (shell, ch 3, shell, ch 2) in each of next 2 ch-3 sps, (shell, ch 3) in same ch-3 sp as first dc, join in 3rd ch of beg ch-3. *(6 shells, 3 ch-3 sps, 3 ch-2 sps)*

Rnd 3: *Sl st in next dc, ch 1, shell in ch-2 sp, ch 1, sk 1 dc, sl st in next dc, ch 1, (shell, ch 3, shell) in next ch-3 sp, ch 1, sk 1 dc, rep from * twice, join in first sl st. Do not fasten off. *(9 shells)*

Tree Trunk

Row 1: Sl st in ch-1 sp, ch 1, sc in same ch-1 sp, sc in next dc, **sc dec** *(see Stitch Guide)* in next 2 dc, sc in next ch-1 sp, turn. *(4 sc)*

Row 2: Ch 1, sc in each of next 4 sc, turn.

Row 3: Rep row 2. Fasten off.

Star

Rnd 1 (RS): With off-white, ch 6, **join** *(see Pattern Notes)* in first ch to form a ring, (**ch 3**—*see Pattern Notes*, 2 dc) in ring, ch 3, (**shell**—*see Special Stitches*, ch 3) 4 times in ring, join in 3rd ch of beg ch-3. *(5 shells, 5 ch-3 sps)*

Rnd 2: Sl st in next ch-3 sp, (ch 3, 2 dc, ch 3, shell) in same sp, ch 1, (shell, ch 3, shell, ch 1) in each of next 4 ch-3 sps, join in 3rd ch of beg ch-3. *(10 shells, 5 ch-3 sps, 5 ch-1 sps)*

Rnd 3: Sl st in next ch-3 sp, (ch 3, 3 dc, ch 3, 4 dc) in same ch-3 sp, ch 1, sl st in next ch-1 sp, ch 1, *(4 dc, ch 3, 4 dc) in next ch-3 sp, ch 1, sl st in next ch-1 sp, ch 1, rep from * 3 times, join in 3rd ch of beg ch-3. Fasten off. ●

Photo Frame

Skill Level

 EASY

Finished Measurement

5¼ inches in diameter

Materials

- Medium (worsted) weight acrylic/wool yarn:
  1 oz/80 yds/40g each red-and-green variegated and off-white
- Size H/8/5mm crochet hook or size needed to obtain gauge
- Yarn needle
- 2½-inch diameter thin bangle bracelet
- Craft glue
- Photo

See page 45 for Yarn Specifics.

Gauge

Rnds 1–3 = 1⅜ inches

Pattern Notes

Weave in loose ends as work progresses.

Join with slip stitch as indicated unless otherwise stated.

Special Stitch

Picot: Ch 3, sl st in first ch of ch-3.

Photo Frame

Rnd 1 (RS): Join desired color with **sl st around ring** *(see illustration)*, ch 1, work 60 sc around bracelet, **join** *(see Pattern Notes)* in beg sc. *(60 sc)*

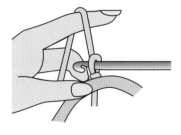

Slip Stitch Around Ring

Rnd 2: Ch 1, sc in each sc around, join in beg sc.

Rnd 3: Ch 1, *sk next 2 sc, (3 dc, **picot**—*see Special Stitch*, 3 dc) in next sc, ch 1, sk next 2 sc, sl st in next sc, ch 1, rep from * 9 times, join in same st as beg ch-1. Fasten off. *(10 shells)*

Finishing
Cut photo to 3 inches in diameter, glue to center
back of Frame. ●

Home

Family Favorite Blanket

Skill Level

 EASY

Finished Measurements

47 inches wide x 61¾ inches long

Materials

- Medium (worsted) weight acrylic/wool yarn:
    - 10½ oz/600 yds/300g each red, dark green and off-white
    - 7 oz/400 yds/200g each #0137 dark pink and pale green
    - 3½ oz/200 yds/100g each pale pink and red-and-green variegated
- Size H/8/5mm crochet hook or size needed to obtain gauge
- Yarn needle

See page 45 for Yarn Specifics.

Gauge

Rnds 1–4 = 4 inches square; finished Block = 13 inches square

Pattern Notes

Weave in loose ends as work progresses.

Join with slip stitch as indicated unless otherwise stated.

Chain-3 at beginning of round counts as first double crochet unless otherwise stated.

Special Stitches

Beginning shell (beg shell): (**Ch 3**—*see Pattern Notes*, 2 dc) in indicated st or sp.

Shell: 3 dc in indicated st or sp.

Corner shell: (3 dc, ch 2, 3 dc) in indicated st or sp.

Color Sequence

Blocks 1 & 9

Work 4 Small Squares each as follows:

A. 2 rnds dark pink, 1 rnd each variegated and off-white.

B. 1 rnd each pale pink, dark pink, pale green and dark green.

C. 1 rnd each dark pink, red, pale green and dark green.

D. 2 rnds pale pink, 1 rnd each variegated and off-white.

Block Edging: Work 1 rnd each red, dark pink, red, off-white and dark green.

Blocks 2, 4, 6, 8, 10 & 12

Work 4 Small Squares each as follows:

A. 1 rnd each red, dark pink, variegated and off-white.

B. 1 rnd each dark green, dark pink, pale green and dark green.

C. 1 rnd each dark pink, pale pink, pale green and dark green.

D. 1 rnd each pale pink, red, variegated and off-white.

Block Edging: Work 1 rnd each red, pale pink, red, dark green and off-white.

Blocks 3 & 7

Work 4 Small Squares each as follows:

A. 2 rnds pale pink, 1 rnd each pale green and dark green.

B. 1 rnd each dark green, pale pink, variegated and off-white.

C. 1 rnd each red, pale pink, variegated and off-white.

D. 2 rnds dark pink, 1 rnd each pale green and dark green.

Block Edging: Work 1 rnd each red, dark pink, red, off-white and dark green.

Blocks 5 & 11

Work 1 Large Square each as follows:

A. 2 rnds each red and dark pink.

B. 1 rnd dark green.

C. 3 rnds pale green.

D. 1 rnd each red, dark pink, red, off-white and dark green.

Blanket

Small Square
Make a total of 40 referring to Color Sequence.

Rnd 1 (RS): With first color, ch 4, **join** (see Pattern Notes) in first ch to form a ring, **beg shell** (see Special Stitches) in ring, ch 2, (**shell**—see Special Stitches in ring, ch 2) 3 times in ring, join in 3rd ch of beg ch-3. Fasten off if new color is required. (4 shells, 4 ch-2 sps)

Rnd 2 (RS): Sl st in each of next 2 dc and next ch-2 sp or join next color in any ch-2 sp, (beg shell, ch 2, shell) in same ch-2 sp, ch 1, [**corner shell** (see Special Stitches) in next ch-2 sp, ch 1] 3 times, join in 3rd ch of beg ch-3. Fasten off if new color is required. (4 corner shells, 4 ch-1 sps)

Rnd 3 (RS): Sl st in each of next 2 dc and next ch-2 sp or join next color in any ch-2 sp, (beg shell, ch 2, shell) in same ch-2 sp, ch 1, shell in next ch-1 sp, ch 1, [corner shell in next corner ch-2 sp, ch 1, shell in next ch-1 sp, ch 1] around, join in 3rd ch of beg ch-3. Fasten off if new color is required. (4 corner shells, 4 shells, 8 ch-1 sps)

Rnd 4 (RS): Sl st in each of next 2 dc and next ch-2 sp or join next color in any ch-2 sp, (beg shell, ch 2, shell) in same ch-2 sp, ch 1, [shell in next ch-1 sp, ch 1] across to next corner ch-2, *corner shell in next ch-2 sp, ch 1, [shell in next ch-1 sp, ch 1] across to next corner ch-2, rep from * around, join in 3rd ch of beg ch-3. Fasten off. (4 corner shells, 8 shells, 12 ch-1 sps)

Block Assembly
Arrange Small Squares as shown in Placement Diagram. Holding Small Squares with RS facing, **whipstitch edges** (see illustration) of squares tog.

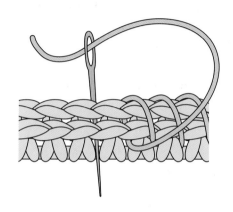

Whipstitch Edges

Block Edging
Note: This is worked around outer edge of 4 joined Small Squares. Change color referring to Color Sequence.

Rnd 1 (RS): Join first color in any ch-2 sp, (beg shell, ch 2, shell) in same ch-2 sp, ch 1, *[shell, ch 1] in each of next 3 ch-1 sps, dc in next corner ch-2 sp, **dc dec** (see Stitch Guide) in same corner ch-2 sp and next corner ch-2 sp, dc in same ch-2 corner (counts as a shell), ch 1, [shell, ch 1] in each of next 3 ch-1 sps**, corner shell in next corner ch-2 sp, ch 1, rep from * around, ending last rep at **, join in 3rd ch of beg ch-3. Fasten off. (4 corner shells, 28 shells, 32 ch-1 sps)

Rnd 2 (RS): Join next color in any ch-2 sp, (beg shell, ch 3, shell) in same ch-2 sp, ch 1, *[shell, ch 1] in each ch-1 sp to next corner ch-2 sp**, corner shell in next corner ch-2 sp, ch 1, rep from * around, ending last rep at **, join in 3rd ch of beg ch-3. (4 corner shells, 32 shells, 36 ch-1 sps)

Rnds 3–5: Rep rnd 2. *(4 corner shells, 44 shells, 4 ch-2 sps, 48 ch-1 sps)*

Large Square

Make 2 referring to Color Sequence.

Rnds 1–4: Rep rnds 1–4 of Small Square.

Rnds 5–13: Rep rnd 4 of Small Square. *(4 corner shells, 44 shells, 48 ch-1 sps)*

Blanket Assembly

Arrange the 12 Blocks as shown in Placement Diagram. With RS facing, whipstitch Blocks tog.

Blanket Edging

Rnd 1 (RS): Join pale green in any corner ch-2 sp, (beg shell, ch 2, shell) in corner ch-2 sp, ch 1, (shell, ch 1) in each ch-1 sp and *[in next Block seam, dc in next ch-2 sp before seam, dc dec in same ch-2 sp and next ch-2 sp after seam, dc in same ch-2 sp as last leg of dec *(counts as a shell)*, ch 1, (shell, ch 1) in each ch-1 sp] across to next corner ch-2 sp**, (corner shell, ch 1) in corner ch-2 sp, (shell, ch 1) in each ch-1 sp, rep from * around, ending last rep at **, join in 3rd ch of beg ch-3. Fasten off. *(4 corner shells, 182 ch-1 sps, 51 shells each long side, 38 shells each short side)*

Rnd 2: Join dark green in any corner ch-2 sp, (beg shell, ch 2, shell) in corner ch-2 sp, ch 1, *[shell in ch-1 sp, ch 1] across to next corner ch-2 sp**, corner shell in corner ch-2 sp, ch 1, rep from * around, ending last rep at **, join in 3rd ch of beg ch-3. *(4 corner shells, 182 shells, 186 ch-1 sps)*

Rnd 3: Sl st in each of next 2 dc, sl st in next ch-2 sp, rep rnd 2 from beg shell. Fasten off. *(4 corner shells, 186 shells, 190 ch-1 sps)*

Rnds 4 & 5: Join off-white, rep rnds 2 and 3. *(4 corner shells, 194 shells, 198 ch-1 sps)*

Rnds 6 & 7: Join red, rep rnds 2 and 3. *(4 corner shells, 202 shells, 206 ch-1 sps)* ●

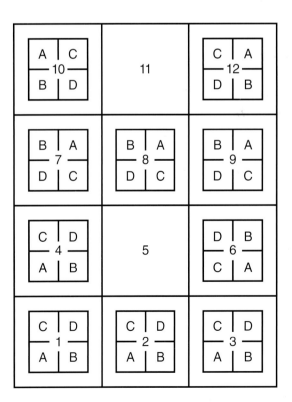

Family Favorite Blanket
Placement Diagram

Bright & Happy Pillow

Skill Level

 EASY

Finished Measurement

14 inches square, including Border

Materials

- Medium (worsted) weight acrylic/wool yarn: 3½ oz/200 yds/100g each dark green, dark pink, off-white, red, pale green, dark blue, pale yellow, bright yellow, bright orange, lime green and pale blue

- Size H/8/5mm crochet hook or size needed to obtain gauge
- Yarn needle
- 14-inch-square pillow form

Note: See page 45 for Yarn Specifics.

Gauge

Rnds 1–3 of Square = 3¼ inches; finished Front/Back = 13 inches square

Pattern Notes

Weave in loose ends as work progresses.

Join with slip stitch as indicated unless otherwise stated.

Chain-3 at beginning of round counts as first double crochet unless otherwise stated.

Special Stitches

Beginning shell (beg shell): (Ch 3—*see Pattern Notes*, 2 dc) in indicated st or sp.

Shell: 3 dc in indicated st or sp.

Corner shell: (3 dc, ch 2, 3 dc) in indicated st or sp.

Picot: Ch 3, sl st in 3rd ch from hook.

Border shell: (Sl st, ch 2, dc, **picot**—*see Special Stitches*, dc, ch 2, sl st) in indicated st or sp.

Color Sequence

Front

Make 1 Large Square each as follows:

A. 1 rnd each pale yellow, pale blue, dark pink, pale green and red.

B. 1 rnd each dark blue, lime green, bright orange, bright yellow and dark green.

C. 1 rnd each lime green, bright orange, dark blue, bright yellow and dark green.

D. 1 rnd each dark pink, pale yellow, pale blue, pale green and red.

Border: 1 rnd each off-white, red, dark green and red.

Back

Make 1 Small Square each as follows:

A. 1 rnd each red, lime green and dark green.

B. 1 rnd each dark green, pale yellow and dark blue.

C. 1 rnd each dark blue, dark pink and pale yellow.

D. 1 rnd each dark green, bright yellow and red.

E. 1 rnd each pale blue, red and off-white.

F. 1 rnd each off-white, dark green and red.

G. 1 rnd each dark pink, off-white and pale blue.

H. 1 rnd each lime green, bright orange and bright yellow.

I. 1 rnd each pale yellow, red and lime green.

Border: 1 rnd each off-white, dark green, red and dark green

Pillow

Front

Large Square
Make 4 referring to Color Sequence.

Rnds 1–3 (RS): Rep rnds 1–3 of Small Square on page 26.

Rnd 4: Join next color in any ch-2 sp, (beg shell, ch 2, shell) in same ch-2 sp, ch 1, [shell in next ch-1 sp, ch 1] across to next corner ch-2 sp, *corner shell in next ch-2 sp, ch 1, [shell in next ch-1 sp, ch 1] across to next corner ch-2 sp, rep from * around, join in 3rd ch of beg ch-3. Fasten off. *(4 corner shells, 8 shells, 12 ch-1 sps)*

Rnd 5: Rep rnd 4. Fasten off. *(4 corner shells, 12 shells, 16 ch-1 sps)*

Assembly
Arrange Squares as indicated in Front Placement Diagram. With RS of Squares facing, **whipstitch edges** *(see illustration)* of Squares tog.

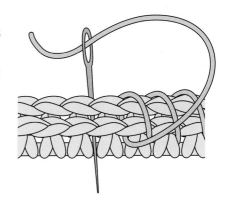

Whipstitch Edges

Border
Work as for Back Border on page 26 referring to Color Sequence.

Assembly

Arrange Squares as indicated in Front Placement Diagram. With RS of Squares facing, whipstitch edges of Squares tog.

Border

Note: Work referring to Color Sequence.

Rnd 1: Join next color in any ch-2 sp, (beg shell, ch 3, shell) in same ch-2 sp, ch 1, *[shell, ch 1] in each ch-1 sp and each ch-2 sp to next corner ch-2 sp**, corner shell in next ch-2 sp, rep from * 3 times, ending last rep at **, join in 3rd ch of beg ch-3. Fasten off. *(4 corner shells, 40 shells, 44 ch-1 sps)*

Rnd 2: Join next color in any ch-2 sp, (beg shell, ch 3, shell, ch 1) in same ch-2 sp, *[shell, ch 1] in each ch-1 sp to next corner ch-2 sp**, (corner shell, ch 1) in next corner ch-2 sp, rep from * around, ending last rep at **, join in 3rd ch of beg ch-3. Fasten off. *(4 corner shells, 44 shells, 48 ch-1 sps)*

Rnds 3 & 4: Rep rnd 2. *(4 corner shells, 52 shells, 56 ch-1 sps)*

Pillow Edging

With WS of Front and Back tog, working through both thicknesses, join dark green in any ch-2 corner sp, *work 2 **border shells** *(see Special Stitches)* in corner ch-2 sp, work 1 border shell in each ch-1 sp to next corner ch-2 sp**, rep from * twice *(3 sides completed)*, insert pillow form, rep from * once, ending rep at **, join in beg sl st. Fasten off. ●

Back

Small Square
Make 9 referring to Color Sequence.

Rnd 1 (RS): With first color, ch 4, **join** *(see Pattern Notes)* in first ch to form a ring, **beg shell** *(see Special Stitches)* in ring, ch 2, (**shell**—*see Special Stitches*, ch 2) 3 times in ring, join in 3rd ch of beg ch-3. Fasten off. *(4 shells, 4 ch-2 sps)*

Rnd 2: Join next color in any ch-2 sp, beg shell in ch-2 sp, ch 2, shell in same ch-2 sp, ch 1, [**corner shell** *(see Special Stitches)* in next ch-2 sp, ch 1] 3 times, join in 3rd ch of beg ch-3. Fasten off. *(4 corner shells, 4 ch-1 sps)*

Rnd 3: Join next color in any ch-2 sp, (beg shell, ch 2, shell) in same ch-2 sp, ch 1, shell in next ch-1 sp, ch 1, [corner shell in next corner ch-2 sp, ch 1, shell in next ch-1 sp, ch 1] around, join in 3rd ch of beg ch-3. Fasten off. *(4 corner shells, 4 shells, 8 ch-1 sps)*

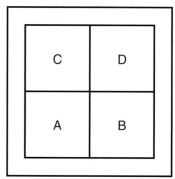

Bright & Happy Pillow
Front Placement Diagram

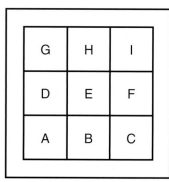

Bright & Happy Pillow
Back Placement Diagram

Winter Warmer Mug Cozy

Skill Level
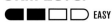 EASY

Finished Measurements
4½ inches wide x 13¾ inches long

Materials
- Medium (worsted) weight acrylic/wool yarn: 3½ oz/200 yds/100g each red, dark pink, dark green and off-white
- Size H/8/5mm crochet hook or size needed to obtain gauge
- Tapestry needle
- 15mm red button

Note: *See page 45 for Yarn Specifics.*

Gauge
Rnds 1–4 of Square Motif = 4 inches square

Pattern Notes
Weave in loose ends as work progresses.

Join with slip stitch as indicated unless otherwise stated.

Chain-3 at beginning of round counts as first double crochet unless otherwise stated.

Special Stitches
Beginning shell (beg shell): (**Ch 3**—*see Pattern Notes*, 2 dc) in indicated st or sp.

Shell: 3 dc in indicated st or sp.

Corner shell: (3 dc, ch 2, 3 dc) in indicated st or sp.

Mug Cozy

Square Motif
Make 2.

Rnd 1 (RS): With red, ch 4, **join** *(see Pattern Notes)* in first ch to form a ring, **beg shell** *(see Special Stitches)* in ring, ch 2, (**shell**—*see Special Stitches*, ch 2) 3 times in ring, join in 3rd ch of beg ch-3. Fasten off. *(4 shells, 4 ch-2 sps)*

Rnd 2 (RS): Join dark pink in any ch-2 sp, (beg shell, ch 2, shell) in same ch-2 sp, ch 1, [**corner shell** *(see Special Stitches)* in next ch-2 sp, ch 1] 3 times, join in 3rd ch of beg ch-3. Fasten off. *(4 corner shells, 4 ch-1 sps)*

Rnd 3 (RS): Join dark green in any ch-2 corner sp, (beg shell, ch 2, shell) in same ch-2 sp, ch 1, shell in next ch-1 sp, ch 1, [corner shell in next ch-2 sp, ch 1, shell in next ch-1 sp, ch 1] 3 times, join in 3rd ch of beg ch-3. Fasten off. *(4 corner shells, 4 shells, 8 ch-1 sps)*

Rnd 4 (RS): Join off-white in any ch-2 sp, (beg shell, ch 2, shell) in same ch-2 sp, ch 1, [shell in next ch-1 sp, ch 1] across to next corner ch-2, *corner shell in next ch-2 sp, ch 1, [shell in next ch-1 sp, ch 1] across to next corner ch-2 sp, rep from * around, join in 3rd ch of beg ch-3. Fasten off. *(4 corner shells, 8 shells, 12 ch-1 sps)*

Triangle Motif

Rnd 1 (RS): With red, ch 4, join in first ch to form a ring, beg shell in ring, ch 2, (shell, ch 2) twice in ring, join in 3rd ch of beg ch-3. Fasten off. *(3 shells, 3 ch-2 sps)*

Rnd 2 (RS): Join dark pink in any ch-2 sp, (beg shell, ch 2, shell) in same ch-2 sp, ch 1, [corner shell in next ch-2 sp, ch 1] twice, join in 3rd ch of beg ch-3. Fasten off. *(3 corner shells, 3 ch-1 sps)*

Rnd 3 (RS): Join dark green in any corner ch-2 sp, (beg shell, ch 2, shell) in same ch-2 sp, ch 1, shell in next ch-1 sp, ch 1, [corner shell in next ch-2 sp, ch 1, shell in next ch-1 sp, ch 1] twice, join in 3rd ch of beg ch-3. Fasten off. *(3 corner shells, 3 shells, 6 ch-1 sps)*

Rnd 4 (RS): Join off-white in any ch-2 sp, (beg shell, ch 2, shell) in same ch-2 sp, ch 1, [shell in next ch-1 sp, ch 1] across to next corner ch-2 sp, *corner shell in next ch-2 sp, ch 1, [shell in next ch-1 sp, ch 1] across to next corner ch-2, rep from * around, join in 3rd ch of beg ch-3. Fasten off. *(3 corner shells, 6 shells, 9 ch-1 sps)*

Assembly

With RS facing, **whipstitch edges** *(see illustration)* of 2 Square Motifs tog to form rectangle, whipstitch Triangle Motif at end of rectangle.

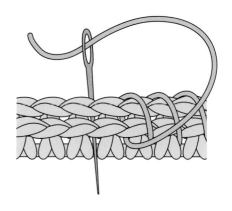

Whipstitch Edges

Edging

With RS facing, join dark pink in corner ch-2 sp of Square and working across end of Cozy, ch 1, 2 sc in same ch-2 sp, [sc in each of next dc and each ch-1 sp to next corner ch-2 sp, 2 sc in next corner ch-2 sp, [working up side edge of Cozy, sc in each dc and each ch-1 sp to seam between Squares, sc in each of next 2 ch-2 sps] twice, sc in each dc and each ch-1 sp to next corner ch-2 sp of triangle, (sc, ch 4, sc) in corner ch-2 sp *(buttonhole lp)*, [working down side edge of Cozy, sc in each dc and each ch-1 sp to seam between Squares, sc in each of next 2 ch-2 sps] twice, sc in each dc and each ch-1 sp to beg sc sts of corner, join in beg sc. Fasten off.

Finishing

With a length of yarn and tapestry needle, sew button to center of rnd 1 of first Square at opposite end of Cozy from Triangle Motif.

Wrap Cozy around mug passing Triangle Motif through handle of mug and secure button lp to button. ●

Trivet

Skill Level
 **EASY**

Finished Measurement
7½ inches square

Materials
- Medium (worsted) weight acrylic/wool yarn: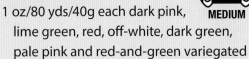
    1 oz/80 yds/40g each dark pink, lime green, red, off-white, dark green, pale pink and red-and-green variegated
- Size H/8/5mm crochet hook or size needed to obtain gauge
- Yarn needle

Note: See page 45 for Yarn Specifics.

Gauge
Rnds 1 and 2 and row 3 = 2¼ inches

Pattern Notes
Weave in loose ends as work progresses.

Join with slip stitch as indicated unless otherwise stated.

Chain-3 at beginning of round counts as first double crochet unless otherwise stated.

Chain-4 at beginning of round counts as first double crochet and chain-1 unless otherwise stated.

Special Stitches
Beginning shell (beg shell): (Ch 3—*see Pattern Notes*, 2 dc) in indicated st or sp.

Shell: 3 dc in indicated st or sp.

Corner shell: (3 dc, ch 2, 3 dc) in indicated st or sp.

Trivet

Rnd 1 (RS): With dark pink, ch 4, **join** *(see Pattern Notes)* in first ch to form a ring, **beg shell** *(see Special Stitches)* in ring, ch 2, (**shell**—*see Special Stitches*, ch 2) 3 times in ring, join in 3rd ch of beg ch-3. *(4 shells, 4 ch-2 sps)*

Rnd 2 (RS): Sl st in next 2 dc, sl st in ch-2 sp, beg shell in ch-2 sp, ch 2, shell in same ch-2 sp, ch 1, [**corner shell** *(see Special Stitches)* in next ch-2 sp, ch 1] 3 times, join in 3rd ch of beg ch-3. Fasten off. *(4 corner shells, 4 ch-1 sps)*

Row 3 (RS): Now working in rows, join lime green in any corner ch-2 sp, beg shell in same ch-2 sp, shell in next ch-1 sp, corner shell in next corner shell, shell in next ch-1 sp, shell in next ch-2 corner sp, turn. *(4 shells, 1 corner shell, 1 ch-2 sp)*

Row 4 (WS): Ch 4 *(see Pattern Notes),* [shell in sp between next 2 shells] twice, corner shell in next corner ch-2 sp, [shell in sp between next 2 shells] twice, ch 1, sk next 2 dc, dc in next dc, fasten off, turn. *(4 shells, 1 corner shell, 2 dc, 2 ch-1 sps)*

Row 5 (RS): Join red in ch-1 sp, beg shell in same ch-1 sp, *[shell in sp between next 2 shells] across to corner ch-2 sp, corner shell in ch-2 sp of corner shell, [shell in sp between next 2 shells] across to last ch-1 sp, shell in ch-1 sp, turn. *(1 corner shell, 6 shells)*

Row 6 (WS): Ch 4, [shell in sp between next 2 shells] across to next corner ch-2 sp, corner shell in ch-2 sp of corner shell, [shell in sp between next 2 shells] across, ending with ch 1, dc in last dc, fasten off, turn. *(1 corner shell, 6 shells, 2 dc, 2 ch-1 sps)*

Row 7 (RS): With off-white, rep row 5. *(1 corner shell, 8 shells)*

Row 8 (WS): Rep row 6. *(1 corner shell, 8 shells, 2 dc, 2 ch-1 sps)*

Row 9 (RS): With dark green, rep row 5. *(1 corner shell, 10 shells)*

Row 10 (WS): Rep row 6. *(1 corner shell, 10 shells, 2 dc, 2 ch-1 sps)*

Row 11 (RS): With pale pink, rep row 5. *(1 corner shell, 12 shells)*

Row 12 (WS): Rep row 6. *(1 corner shell, 12 shells, 2 dc, 2 ch-1 sps)*

Rnd 13 (RS): Now working in rnds, join variegated in corner ch-2 sp of corner shell, (beg shell, ch 2, shell) in corner ch-2 sp, [shell in sp between next 2 shells] 6 times, corner shell in next ch-1 sp of corner, shell in side edge of each dc of rows 10, 8, 6 and 4, shell in corner ch-2 sp of rnd 2, shell in next ch-1 sp, corner shell in next ch-2 sp of next corner shell, shell in next ch-1 sp, shell in ch-2 corner sp, shell in side edge of each dc of rows 4, 6, 8 and 10, corner shell in ch-1 sp of corner, [shell in sp between next 2 shells] 6 times, join in 3rd ch of beg ch-3. Fasten off. *(4 corner shells, 24 shells)* ●

Gifts

Sweet Scarf

Skill Level

 INTERMEDIATE

Finished Measurements

8½ inches wide x 78 inches long

Materials

- Medium (worsted) weight acrylic/wool yarn: 3½ oz/200 yds/100g each dark pink, pale pink, off-white, medium gray and light gray heather

4 MEDIUM

- Size H/8/5mm crochet hook or size needed to obtain gauge
- Yarn needle

Note: *See page 45 for Yarn Specifics.*

Gauge

Rnds 1–3 = 3¼ inches square

Pattern Notes

Weave in loose ends as work progresses.

Join with slip stitch as indicated unless otherwise stated.

Chain-3 at beginning of round counts as first double crochet unless otherwise stated.

Special Stitches

Beginning shell (beg shell): (Ch 3—*see Pattern Notes*, 2 dc) in indicated st or sp.

Shell: 3 dc in indicated st or sp.

Corner shell: (3 dc, ch 2, 3 dc) in indicated st or sp.

Color Sequence

Make 4 Squares each color combination as follows:

Square 1: 1 rnd each off-white, dark pink and medium gray.

Square 2: 2 rnds pale pink, 1 rnd light gray heather.

Square 3: 1 rnd each dark pink, off-white and medium gray.

Square 4: 1 rnd each dark pink, pale pink and light gray heather.

Square 5: 1 rnd each pale pink, off-white and medium gray.

Square 6: 2 rnds dark pink and 1 rnd light gray heather.

Square 7: 2 rnds off-white and 1 rnd medium gray.

Square 8: 1 rnd each pale pink, dark pink and light gray heather.

Square 9: 1 rnd each dark pink, pale pink and medium gray.

Square 10: 1 rnd each pale pink, off-white and light gray heather.

Square 11: 2 rnds pale pink and 1 rnd medium gray.

Square 12: 1 rnd each dark pink, off-white and light gray heather.

Square 13: 2 rnds dark pink and 1 rnd medium gray.

Square 14: 1 rnd each off-white, dark pink and light gray heather.

Square 15: 1 rnd each off-white, pale pink and medium gray.

Square 16: 1 rnd each off-white, pale pink and light gray heather.

Square 17: 1 rnd each pale pink, dark pink and medium gray.

Square 18: 2 rnds off-white and 1 rnd light gray heather.

Scarf

Square
Make 72 referring to Color Sequence.

First Square
Rnd 1 (RS): With first color, ch 4, **join** (see Pattern Notes) in first ch to form a ring, **beg shell** (see Special Stitches) in ring, ch 2, (**shell**—see Special Stitches, ch 2) 3 times in ring, join in 3rd ch of beg ch-3. Fasten off if new color is required. If not fastening off, sl st in next ch-2 sp. (4 shells, 4 ch-2 sps)

Rnd 2 (RS): Join next color in any ch-2 sp or continue with previous rnd color as indicated, beg shell in ch-2 sp, ch 2, shell in same ch-2 sp, ch 1, [**corner shell** (see Special Stitches) in next ch-2 sp, ch 1] 3 times, join in 3rd ch of beg ch-3. Fasten off. (4 corner shells, 4 ch-1 sps)

Rnd 3 (RS): Join next color in any ch-2 sp, (beg shell, ch 2, shell) in same ch-2 sp, ch 1, shell in next ch-1 sp, ch 1, [corner shell in next corner ch-2 sp, ch 1, shell in next ch-1 sp, ch 1] around, join in 3rd ch of beg ch-3. Fasten off. (4 corner shells, 4 shells, 8 ch-1 sps)

1-Sided Joining Square
Rnds 1 & 2 (RS): Rep rnds 1 and 2 of First Square.

Rnd 3: Join next color in any ch-2 sp, (beg shell, ch 1, holding WS of Squares tog, sc in corner sp of adjacent Square, ch 1, shell) in same ch-2 sp, sc in next ch-1 sp of adjacent Square, shell in next ch-1 sp of working Square, sc in next ch-1 sp of adjacent Square, (shell, ch 1, sc in corner ch-2 sp of adjacent Square, ch 1, shell) in corner ch-2 sp, ch 1, complete rnd as for First Square.

2-Sided Joining Square
Rnds 1 & 2 (RS): Rep rnds 1 and 2 of First Square.

Rnd 3: Join next color in any ch-2 sp, (beg shell, ch 1, holding WS of Squares tog, sc in corner sp of adjacent Square, ch 1, shell) in same ch-2 sp, *sc in next ch-1 sp of adjacent Square, shell in next ch-1 sp of working Square, sc in next ch-1 sp of adjacent Square, (shell in corner ch-2 sp, ch 1, sc in corner ch-2 sp of adjacent Square, ch 1, shell in same ch-2 sp)*, rep from * to * once, ch 1, complete rnd as for First Square.

Referring to Placement Diagram, work Squares 1–18 a total of 4 times, joining them as you go into 3 columns of 24 Squares. ●

16	17	18
13	14	15
10	11	12
7	8	9
4	5	6
1	2	3

Sweet Scarf
Placement Diagram
Note: *Rep Placement Diagram 4 times vertically.*

Pixie Hats

Girl's Hat

Skill Level
  EASY

Finished Measurements
8 inches deep x 9 inches tall

Materials
- Medium (worsted) weight acrylic/wool yarn:
  3½ oz/200 yds/100g each medium gray and dark pink
- Size H/8/5mm crochet hook or size needed to obtain gauge
- Yarn needle

Note: See page 45 for Yarn Specifics.

Gauge
Rnds 1–3 = 3¼ inches

Pattern Notes
Weave in loose ends as work progresses.

Join with slip stitch as indicated unless otherwise stated.

Chain-3 at beginning of round counts as first double crochet unless otherwise stated.

Special Stitches
Beginning shell (beg shell): (**Ch 3**—*see Pattern Notes*, 2 dc) in indicated st or sp.

Shell: 3 dc in indicated st or sp.

Corner shell: (3 dc, ch 2, 3 dc) in indicated st or sp.

Hat

Square
Make 2.

Rnd 1 (RS): With medium gray, ch 4, **join** (*see Pattern Notes*) in first ch to form a ring, **beg shell** (*see Special Stitches*) in ring, ch 2, (**shell**—*see Special Stitches*, ch 2) 3 times in ring, join in 3rd ch of beg ch-3. (*4 shells, 4 ch-2 sps*)

Rnd 2 (RS): Sl st in corner ch-2 sp, beg shell in ch-2 sp, ch 2, shell in same ch-2 sp, ch 1, [**corner shell** (see Special Stitches) in next ch-2 sp, ch 1] 3 times, join in 3rd ch of beg ch-3. *(4 corner shells, 4 ch-1 sps)*

Rnd 3 (RS): Sl st in corner ch-2 sp, (beg shell, ch 2, shell) in same ch-2 sp, ch 1, shell in ch-1 sp, ch 1, [corner shell in next corner ch-2 sp, ch 1, shell in next ch-1 sp, ch 1] around, join in 3rd ch of beg ch-3. *(4 corner shells, 4 shells, 8 ch-1 sps)*

Rnd 4 (RS): Sl st in corner ch-2 sp, (beg shell, ch 2, shell) in same ch-2 sp, ch 1, [shell in next ch-1 sp, ch 1] across to next corner ch-2 sp, *corner shell in next ch-2 sp, ch 1, [shell in next ch-1 sp, ch 1] across to next corner ch-2 sp, rep from * around, join in 3rd ch of beg ch-3. *(4 corner shells, 8 shells, 12 ch-1 sps)*

Rnds 5–8: Rep rnd 4. *(4 corner shells, 24 shells, 28 ch-1 sps)*

Assembly
With WS tog, **whipstitch** (see illustration) 2 sides of Squares tog for top and back of Hat.

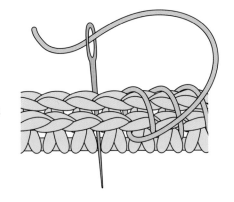

Whipstitch Edges

Edging
Rnd 1 (RS):
Join dark pink in corner ch-2 sp and working toward top of Hat, (beg shell, ch 2, shell) in same corner ch-2 sp, ch 1, *[shell, ch 1] in each of next 7 ch-1 sps, dc in ch-2 sp before seam, dc in seam, dc in next ch-2 sp after seam *(counts as shell)*, [shell, ch 1] in each of next 7 ch-1 sps*, corner shell in next corner ch-2 sp, ch 1, rep from * to *, join in 3rd ch of beg ch-3. Fasten off. *(2 corner shells, 30 shells, 32 ch-1 sps)*

Rnd 2: Join medium gray in any corner ch-2 sp, ch 1, [(2 sc, ch 2, 2 sc) in corner ch-2 sp, sc in each dc to next corner] twice, join in beg sc. Fasten off. *(110 sc, 2 ch-2 sps)*

Rnd 3: Join dark pink in corner ch-2 sp, ch 1, [(2 sc, ch 2, 2 sc) in corner ch-2 sp, sc in each sc to next corner] twice, join in beg sc. Fasten off. *(118 sc, 2 ch-2 sps)*

Tie
Make 2.

Cut 2 40-inch lengths medium gray and 1 40-inch length dark pink. Hold strands tog, fold in half, insert hook in corner ch-2 sp, draw strands through at fold to form a lp on hook, work a chain 12 inches long, leaving 4-inch length, fasten off rem strands.

Baby's Hat

Skill Level
 EASY

Finished Measurements
7 inches deep x 7¼ inches tall

Materials
- Medium (worsted) weight acrylic/wool yarn: 3½ oz/200 yds/100g each lime green, bright orange, pale blue and bright yellow
- Size H/8/5mm crochet hook or size needed to obtain gauge
- Yarn needle

Note: *See page 45 for Yarn Specifics.*

Gauge
Rnds 1–3 = 2½ inches; 9 dc = 1 inch

Pattern Notes
Weave in loose ends as work progresses.

Join with slip stitch as indicated unless otherwise stated.

Chain-3 at beginning of round counts as first double crochet unless otherwise stated.

Special Stitches

Beginning shell (beg shell): (**Ch 3**—*see Pattern Notes*, 2 dc) in indicated st or sp.

Shell: 3 dc in indicated st or sp.

Corner shell: (3 dc, ch 2, 3 dc) in indicated st or sp.

Hat

Square
Make 2.

Rnd 1 (RS): With lime green, ch 4, **join** (*see Pattern Notes*) in first ch to form a ring, **beg shell** (*see Special Stitches*) in ring, ch 2, (**shell**—*see Special Stitches*, ch 2) 3 times in ring, join in 3rd ch of beg ch-3. Fasten off. *(4 shells, 4 ch-2 sps)*

Rnd 2 (RS): Join bright orange in corner ch-2 sp, beg shell in ch-2 sp, ch 2, shell in same ch-2 sp, ch 1, [**corner shell** (*see Special Stitches*) in next ch-2 sp, ch 1] 3 times, join in 3rd ch of beg ch-3. Fasten off. *(4 corner shells, 4 ch-1 sps)*

Rnd 3 (RS): Join pale blue in corner ch-2 sp, (beg shell, ch 2, shell) in same ch-2 sp, ch 1, shell in next ch-1 sp, ch 1, [corner shell in next corner ch-2 sp, ch 1, shell in next ch-1 sp, ch 1] around, join in 3rd ch of beg ch-3. Fasten off. *(4 corner shells, 4 shells, 8 ch-1 sps)*

Rnd 4 (RS): Join bright yellow in corner ch-2 sp, (beg shell, ch 2, shell) in same ch-2 sp, ch 1, [shell in next ch-1 sp, ch 1] across to next corner ch-2 sp, *corner shell in next ch-2 sp, ch 1, [shell in next ch-1 sp, ch 1] across to next corner ch-2 sp, rep from * around, join in 3rd ch of beg ch-3. Fasten off. *(4 corner shells, 8 shells, 12 ch-1 sps)*

Rnd 5: Rep rnd 4 with pale blue. Fasten off. *(4 corner shells, 12 shells, 16 ch-1 sps)*

Rnd 6: Rep rnd 4 with bright orange. Fasten off. *(4 corner shells, 16 shells, 20 ch-1 sps)*

Rnd 7: Rep rnd 4 with lime green. Fasten off. *(4 corner shells, 20 shells, 24 ch-1 sps)*

Assembly
With WS tog, **whipstitch** (*see illustration on page 38*) 2 sides of Squares tog for top and back of Hat.

Edging
Rnd 1 (RS): Join bright yellow in corner ch-2 sp, ch 1, [(2 sc, ch 2, 2 sc) in corner ch-2 sp, sc in each of next 42 dc] twice, join in beg sc. Fasten off. *(92 sc, 2 ch-2 sps)*

Rnd 2: Join pale blue at center back neckline of Hat, ch 1, sc in each sc around, working (2 sc, ch 2, 2 sc) in each corner ch-2 sp, join in beg sc. Fasten off. *(100 sc, 2 ch-2 sps)*

Tie
Make 2.

Cut 2 50-inch lengths pale blue. Hold strands tog, fold in half, insert hook in corner ch-2 sp, draw strands through at fold to form a lp on hook, work a chain 16 inches long, leaving 1-inch length, fasten off. ●

Chill Chaser Wrap

Skill Level

 EASY

Finished Measurements

58 inches wide x 28 inches long, excluding Tassels

Materials

- Medium (worsted) weight acrylic/wool yarn: 3½ oz/200 yds/100g each pale blue, dark blue, light gray heather, bright orange and bright yellow
- Size H/8/5mm crochet hook or size needed to obtain gauge
- Yarn needle

Note: See page 45 for Yarn Specifics.

4 MEDIUM

Gauge

[Shell, ch 1] 4 times = 4 inches; 8 rows = 4 inches

Pattern Notes

Weave in loose ends as work progresses.

Join with slip stitch as indicated unless otherwise stated.

Chain-5 at beginning of row counts as first treble crochet and chain-1 unless otherwise stated.

Chain-3 at beginning of row counts as first double crochet unless otherwise stated.

Special Stitches

Corner shell: (3 dc, ch 2, 3 dc) in indicated st or sp.

Shell: 3 dc in indicated st or sp.

Picot: Ch 3, sl st in 3rd ch from hook.

Wrap

Body

Row 1 (RS): With pale blue, ch 4, **join** (see Pattern Notes) in first ch to form a ring, **ch 5** (see Pattern Notes), **corner shell** (see Special Stitches), ch 1, tr in ring, turn. (2 tr, 1 corner shell, 2 ch-1 sps)

Row 2: Ch 5, (**shell**—see Special Stitches, ch 1) in next ch-1 sp, corner shell in next corner ch-2 sp, ch 1, (shell, ch 1) in next ch-1 sp, tr in 4th ch of beg ch-5, turn. (2 tr, 1 corner shell, 2 shells)

Row 3: Change color (see Stitch Guide) to dark blue, ch 5, (shell, ch 1) in each ch-1 sp to next corner ch-2 sp, corner shell in corner ch-2 sp, ch 1, (shell, ch 1) in each ch-1 sp to last tr, tr in 4th ch of beg ch-5, turn. (2 tr, 1 corner shell, 4 shells)

Row 4: Ch 5, (shell, ch 1) in each ch-1 sp to corner ch-2 sp, corner shell in corner ch-2 sp, ch 1, (shell, ch 1) in each ch-1 sp to last tr, tr in 4th ch of beg ch-5, turn. (2 tr, 1 corner shell, 6 shells)

Row 5: Change color to light gray heather, rep row 4. (2 tr, 1 corner shell, 8 shells)

Rows 6–13: Rep row 4 with 1 row each bright orange, light gray heather, dark blue, bright yellow, pale blue, light gray heather, bright orange and light gray heather. (2 tr, 1 corner shell, 24 shells)

Note: Each row adds 2 shells.

Rows 14 & 15: Rep row 4 with dark blue.

Rows 16–18: Rep row 4 with 1 row each bright yellow, light gray heather and bright orange.

Rows 19–22: Rep row 4 with 2 rows each pale blue and dark blue.

Rows 23–31: Rep row 4 with 1 row each light gray heather, bright orange, light gray heather, dark blue, bright yellow, pale blue, light gray heather, bright orange and light gray heather.

Rows 32 & 33: Rep row 4 with dark blue.

Rows 34–36: Rep row 4 with 1 row each bright yellow, light gray heather and bright orange.

Rows 37 & 38: Rep row 4 with 2 rows pale blue, at the end of last rep, change color to dark blue, fasten off pale blue, turn. *(2 tr, 1 corner shell, 74 shells)*

Edging

Rnd 1 (RS): (**Ch 3**—*see Pattern Notes*, 2 dc, **picot**—*see Special Stitches,* 3 dc, picot) in ch-1 sp, (shell, picot) in each ch-1 sp to corner ch-2 sp, (3 dc, picot, 3 dc) in corner ch-2 sp, picot, (shell, picot) in each ch-1 sp to last ch-1 sp, (shell, picot, shell) in last ch-1 sp, picot, working across top edge of Wrap in ends of rows, (shell, picot) in each tr and in beg ch-4 sp, join in 3rd ch of beg ch-3. Fasten off. *(3 corner shells, 149 shells)*

Tassel
Make 2.

With dark blue, cut 15 strands each 18 inches long. Hold all strands tog, fold in half at center, insert hook in corner ch-2 sp at top edge of Wrap, fold strands in half and draw through corner ch-2 sp to form a lp on hook, draw ends of strand through lp on hook, pull gently to secure. Attach 2nd Tassel to opposite top corner of Wrap. ●

Family Mitts

Skill Level

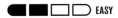 EASY

Finished Measurements

Small: 3¼ inches wide x 5½ inches long

Medium: 4 inches wide x 6 inches long

Large: 5 inches wide x 7 inches long

Materials

- Medium (worsted) weight acrylic/wool yarn:
  3½ oz/200 yds/100g each dark blue, bright yellow, red, lime green, pale blue, light gray heather, bright orange and medium gray
- Size H/8/5mm crochet hook or size needed to obtain gauge
- Yarn needle

Note: See page 45 for Yarn Specifics.

Gauge

Rnds 1–3 = 3¼ inches

Pattern Notes

Weave in loose ends as work progresses.

Join with slip stitch as indicated unless otherwise stated.

Chain-3 at beginning of round counts as first double crochet unless otherwise stated.

Special Stitches

Beginning shell (beg shell): (Ch 3—*see Pattern Notes*, 2 dc) in indicated st or sp.

Shell: 3 dc in indicated st or sp.

Corner shell: (3 dc, ch 2, 3 dc) in indicated st or sp.

Pattern Stitch

Body Square

Rnd 1 (RS): With first color, ch 4, **join** *(see Pattern Notes)* in first ch to form a ring, **beg shell** *(see Special Stitches)* in ring, ch 2, (**shell**—*see Special Stitches* in ring, ch 2) 3 times in ring, join in 3rd ch of beg ch-3. Fasten off. *(4 shells, 4 ch-2 sps)*

Rnd 2 (RS): Join next color in any ch-2 sp, beg shell in ch-2 sp, ch 2, shell in same ch-2 sp, ch 1, [**corner shell** *(see Special Stitches)* in next ch-2 sp, ch 1] 3 times, join in 3rd ch of beg ch-3. Fasten off. *(4 corner shells, 4 ch-1 sps)*

Rnd 3 (RS): Join next color in any ch-2 sp, (beg shell, ch 2, shell) in same ch-2 sp, ch 1, shell in ch-1 sp, ch 1, [corner shell in next corner ch-2 sp, ch 1, shell in next ch-1 sp, ch 1] around, join in 3rd ch of beg ch-3. Fasten off. *(4 corner shells, 4 shells, 8 ch-1 sps)*

Rnd 4 (RS): Join next color in any ch-2 sp, (beg shell, ch 2, shell) in same ch-2 sp, ch 1, [shell in next ch-1 sp, ch 1] across to next corner ch-2, *corner shell in next ch-2 sp, ch 1, [shell in next ch-1 sp, ch 1] across to next corner ch-2, rep from * around, join in 3rd ch of beg ch-3. Fasten off. *(4 corner shells, 8 shells, 12 ch-1 sps)*

Rnd 5: Join next color in any ch-2 corner sp, rep rnd 4. Fasten off. *(4 corner shells, 12 shells 16 ch-1 sps)*

Small Mitts

Body Square

Make 4.

Rnds 1–3 (RS): Work rnds 1–3 of Pattern Stitch working 1 rnd each dark blue, bright yellow and red.

With WS of 2 Squares tog, **whipstitch edges** *(see illustration on page 44)* across side edge. Whipstitch

opposite side edge leaving last 3 dc of corner shell *(3 sts total)* unsewn for thumb opening.

Finger Band

Rnd 1 (RS): Join lime green in side seam, ch 1, work 24 sc evenly sp around opening, join in beg sc. Fasten off. *(24 sc)*

Rnd 2: Join bright orange in any sc, ch 1, sc in each sc around, join in beg sc. Fasten off.

Rnd 3: Rep rnd 2 with pale blue.

Rnd 4: Rep rnd 2 with lime green.

Wristband

Rnds 1 & 2 (RS): Rep rnds 1 and 2 of Finger Band.

Rnds 3 & 4: Join pale blue, in any sc, ch 1, sc in each sc around, join in beg sc. At the end of rnd 4, fasten off.

Rnds 5 & 6: Join lime green, rep rnds 3 and 4.

Medium Mitts

Body Square
Make 4.

Rnds 1–4 (RS): Work rnds 1–4 of Pattern Stitch, working 1 rnd each pale blue, light gray heather, pale blue and medium gray.

With WS of 2 Squares tog, **whipstitch edges** (see illustration) across side edge. Whipstitch opposite side edge corner shell, ch 1 sp and next 3 dc, leaving next ch-1 sp and 3 dc (4 sts total) unsewn for opening of thumb.

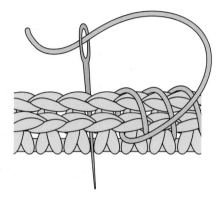

Whipstitch Edges

Finger Band
Rnd 1 (RS): Join light gray heather in side seam, ch 1, work 28 sc evenly sp around opening, join in beg sc. Fasten off. (28 sc)

Rnd 2: Join medium gray in any sc, ch 1, sc in each sc around, join in beg sc. Fasten off.

Rnd 3: Rep rnd 2 with pale blue.

Rnd 4: Rep rnd 2 with medium gray.

Wristband
Rnds 1 & 2 (RS): Rep rnds 1 and 2 of Finger Band.

Rnd 3: Join light gray heather in side seam, ch 1, sc in each sc around opening, join in beg sc. Fasten off.

Rnd 4: Join medium gray in any sc, ch 1, sc in each sc around, join in beg sc. Fasten off.

Rnd 5: Join pale blue, rep rnd 4.

Rnd 6: Join medium gray, rep rnd 4.

Large Mitts

Body Square
Make 4.

Rnds 1–5 (RS): Work rnds 1–5 of Pattern Stitch working 1 rnd each red, medium gray, red, light gray heather and medium gray.

With WS of 2 Squares tog, **whipstitch edges** (see illustration) across side edge. Whipstitch opposite side edge corner shell, ch-1 sp and next 3 dc, leaving next ch-1 sp, 3 dc and ch-1 sp (5 sts total) unsewn for thumb opening.

Finger Band
Rnd 1 (RS): Join light gray heather in side seam, ch 1, work 32 sc evenly sp around opening, join in beg sc. Fasten off. (32 sc)

Rnd 2: Join medium gray in any sc, ch 1, sc in each sc around, join in beg sc. Fasten off.

Rnd 3: Rep rnd 2 with red.

Rnd 4: Rep rnd 2 with medium gray.

Wristband
Rnds 1 & 2 (RS): Rep rnds 1 and 2 of Finger Band.

Rnd 3: Join light gray heather in side seam, ch 1, sc in each sc around opening, join in beg sc. Fasten off.

Rnd 4: Join medium gray in any sc, ch 1, sc in each sc around, join in beg sc. Fasten off.

Rnd 5: Join red, rep rnd 4.

Rnd 6: Join medium gray, rep rnd 4. ●

YARN SPECIFICS

The projects in this book were made using Plymouth Yarn Encore Worsted medium (worsted) weight yarn. Please refer to the specific project instructions for the yarn colors used, recommended gauge and the amount required. Below we have listed the yarn used for our photography models as well as appropriate substitutes.

Cheerful Tree Skirt

- Plymouth Yarn Encore Worsted medium (worsted) weight acrylic/wool yarn (3½ oz/200 yds/ 100g per skein):
    - 3 skeins each #0475 stitch red and #0146 winter white
    - 2 skeins each #0054 Christmas green and #3335 Rio lime

Merry Stocking

- Plymouth Yarn Encore Worsted medium (worsted) weight acrylic/wool yarn (3½ oz/200 yds/ 100g per skein):
    - 1 skein each #1001 merry, #0475 stitch red, #0146 winter white and #0054 Christmas green

Garland

- Plymouth Encore Worsted medium (worsted) weight acrylic/wool yarn (3½ oz/200 yds/ 100g per skein):
    - 1 skein each #1001 merry, #0475 stitch red, #0146 winter white #0054 Christmas green #1383 bright orange, #4045 serenity blue, #3335 Rio lime, #0450 green and #0449 pink

Keepsake Ornaments

- Plymouth Yarn Encore Worsted medium (worsted) weight acrylic/wool yarn (3½ oz/200 yds/ 100g per skein):
    - 25 yds each #0054 Christmas green, #0475 stitch red, #3335 Rio lime and #0146 winter white

Photo Frame

- Plymouth Yarn Encore Worsted medium (worsted) weight acrylic/wool yarn (3½ oz/200 yds/ 100g per skein):
    - 1 oz each #1001 merry and #0146 winter white

Family Favorite Blanket

- Plymouth Yarn Encore Worsted medium (worsted) weight acrylic/wool yarn (3½ oz/200 yds/ 100g per skein):
    - 3 skeins each #0475 stitch red, #0054 Christmas green and #0146 winter white
    - 2 skeins each #0137 California pink and #0450 green
    - 1 skein each #0449 pink and #1001 merry

Bright & Happy Pillow

- Plymouth Yarn Encore Worsted medium (worsted) weight acrylic/wool yarn (3½ oz/200 yds/ 100g per skein):
    - 1 skein each #0054 Christmas green, #0137 California pink, #0146 winter white, #0475 stitch red, #0450 green, #0133 royal, #0215 yellow, #1382 bright yellow, #1383 bright orange, #3335 Rio lime and #4045 serenity blue

Winter Warmer Mug Cozy

- Plymouth Yarn Encore Worsted medium (worsted) weight acrylic/wool yarn (3½ oz/200 yds/ 100g per skein):
    - 1 skein each #0475 stitch red, #0137 California pink, #0054 Christmas green and #0146 winter white

Trivet

- Plymouth Yarn Encore Worsted medium (worsted) weight acrylic/wool yarn (3½ oz/200 yds/ 100g per skein):
    - 1 oz each #0137 California pink, #3335 Rio lime, #0475 stitch red, #0146 winter white, #0054 Christmas green, #0449 pink and #1001 merry

Sweet Scarf
- Plymouth Yarn Encore Worsted medium (worsted) weight acrylic/wool yarn (3½ oz/200 yds/ 100g per skein):
    1 skein each #0137 California pink, #0449 pink, #0146 winter white, #0194 medium grey and #6007 light grey heather

Pixie Hats (Girl's)
- Plymouth Yarn Encore Worsted medium (worsted) weight acrylic/wool yarn (3½ oz/200 yds/ 100g per skein):
    1 skeins each #0194 medium grey and #0137 California pink

Pixie Hats (Baby's)
- Plymouth Yarn Encore Worsted medium (worsted) weight acrylic/wool yarn (3½ oz/200 yds/ 100g per skein):
    1 skein each #3335 Rio lime, #1383 bright orange, #4045 serenity blue and #1382 bright yellow

Chill Chaser Wrap
- Plymouth Yarn Encore Worsted medium (worsted) weight acrylic/wool yarn (3½ oz/200 yds/ 100g per skein):
    1 skein each #4045 serenity blue, #0133 royal, #6007 light grey heather, #1383 bright orange and #1382 bright yellow

Family Mitts
- Plymouth Yarn Encore Worsted medium (worsted) weight acrylic/wool yarn (3½ oz/200 yds/ 100g per skein):
    1 skein each #0133 royal, #1382 bright yellow, #0475 stitch red, #3335 Rio lime #4045 serenity blue, #6007 light grey heather, #1383 bright orange and #0194 medium grey

YARN SUBSTITUTES
- Caron Simply Soft
- Premier Yarns Deborah Norville Everyday Soft Worsted
- Premier Yarns Ever Soft Worsted
- Red Heart Super Saver

STITCH GUIDE

STITCH ABBREVIATIONS

beg .... begin/begins/beginning
bpdc .... back post double crochet
bpsc .... back post single crochet
bptr............................. back post treble crochet
CC .... contrasting color
ch(s) ....chain(s)
ch- .... refers to chain or space
    previously made (i.e., ch-1 space)
ch sp(s) .... chain space(s)
cl(s) .... cluster(s)
cm .... centimeter(s)
dc.................... double crochet (singular/plural)
dc dec........................ double crochet 2 or more
    stitches together, as indicated
dec..................... decrease/decreases/decreasing
dtr .... double treble crochet
ext ....extended
fpdc........................... front post double crochet
fpsc .... front post single crochet
fptr .... front post treble crochet
g ....gram(s)
hdc .... half double crochet
hdc dec.................. half double crochet 2 or more
    stitches together, as indicated
inc .... increase/increases/increasing
lp(s)...................................loop(s)
MC .... main color
mm ....millimeter(s)
oz .... ounce(s)
pc .... popcorn(s)
rem .... remain/remains/remaining
rep(s) ....repeat(s)
rnd(s) ....round(s)
RS...................................... right side
sc .... single crochet (singular/plural)
sc dec........................single crochet 2 or more
    stitches together, as indicated
sk ....skip/skipped/skipping
sl st(s) .... slip stitch(es)
sp(s) .... space(s)/spaced
st(s) ....stitch(es)
tog...................................together
tr....................................... treble crochet
trtr.................................triple treble
WS .... wrong side
yd(s) ....yard(s)
yo .... yarn over

YARN CONVERSION

OUNCES TO GRAMS	GRAMS TO OUNCES
1 .... 28.4	25 .... ⅞
2 .... 56.7	40 .... 1⅔
3 .... 85.0	50 .... 1¾
4 .... 113.4	100 .... 3½

UNITED STATES		UNITED KINGDOM
sl st (slip stitch)	=	sc (single crochet)
sc (single crochet)	=	dc (double crochet)
hdc (half double crochet)	=	htr (half treble crochet)
dc (double crochet)	=	tr (treble crochet)
tr (treble crochet)	=	dtr (double treble crochet)
dtr (double treble crochet)	=	ttr (triple treble crochet)
skip	=	miss

Single crochet decrease (sc dec):
(Insert hook, yo, draw lp through) in each of the sts indicated, yo, draw through all lps on hook.

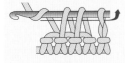

Example of 2-sc dec

Half double crochet decrease (hdc dec):
(Yo, insert hook, yo, draw lp through) in each of the sts indicated, yo, draw through all lps on hook.

Example of 2-hdc dec

Reverse single crochet (reverse sc):
Ch 1, sk first st, working from left to right, insert hook in next st from front to back, draw up lp on hook, yo and draw through both lps on hook.

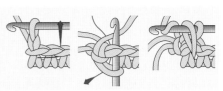

Chain (ch):
Yo, pull through lp on hook.

Single crochet (sc):
Insert hook in st, yo, pull through st, yo, pull through both lps on hook.

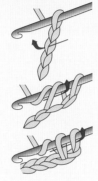

Double crochet (dc):
Yo, insert hook in st, yo, pull through st, [yo, pull through 2 lps] twice.

Double crochet decrease (dc dec):
(Yo, insert hook, yo, draw lp through, yo, draw through 2 lps on hook) in each of the sts indicated, yo, draw through all lps on hook.

Example of 2-dc dec

Front loop (front lp) Back loop (back lp)

Front Loop   Back Loop

Front post stitch (fp): Back post stitch (bp):
When working post st, insert hook from right to left around post of st on previous row.

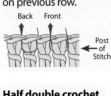

Back Front

Post of Stitch

Half double crochet (hdc):
Yo, insert hook in st, yo, pull through st, yo, pull through all 3 lps on hook.

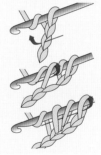

Double treble crochet (dtr):
Yo 3 times, insert hook in st, yo, pull through st, [yo, pull through 2 lps] 4 times.

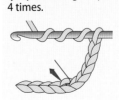

Treble crochet decrease (tr dec):
Holding back last lp of each st, tr in each of the sts indicated, yo, pull through all lps on hook.

Example of 2-tr dec

Slip stitch (sl st):
Insert hook in st, pull through both lps on hook.

Chain color change (ch color change)
Yo with new color, draw through last lp on hook.

Double crochet color change (dc color change)
Drop first color, yo with new color, draw through last 2 lps of st.

Treble crochet (tr):
Yo twice, insert hook in st, yo, pull through st, [yo, pull through 2 lps] 3 times.

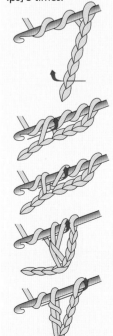

Metric Conversion Charts

METRIC CONVERSIONS

yards	x	.9144	=	metres (m)
yards	x	91.44	=	centimetres (cm)
inches	x	2.54	=	centimetres (cm)
inches	x	25.40	=	millimetres (mm)
inches	x	.0254	=	metres (m)

centimetres	x	.3937	=	inches
metres	x	1.0936	=	yards

INCHES INTO MILLIMETRES & CENTIMETRES (Rounded off slightly)

inches	mm	cm	inches	cm	inches	cm	inches	cm
1/8	3	0.3	5	12.5	21	53.5	38	96.5
1/4	6	0.6	5 1/2	14	22	56	39	99
3/8	10	1	6	15	23	58.5	40	101.5
1/2	13	1.3	7	18	24	61	41	104
5/8	15	1.5	8	20.5	25	63.5	42	106.5
3/4	20	2	9	23	26	66	43	109
7/8	22	2.2	10	25.5	27	68.5	44	112
1	25	2.5	11	28	28	71	45	114.5
1 1/4	32	3.2	12	30.5	29	73.5	46	117
1 1/2	38	3.8	13	33	30	76	47	119.5
1 3/4	45	4.5	14	35.5	31	79	48	122
2	50	5	15	38	32	81.5	49	124.5
2 1/2	65	6.5	16	40.5	33	84	50	127
3	75	7.5	17	43	34	86.5		
3 1/2	90	9	18	46	35	89		
4	100	10	19	48.5	36	91.5		
4 1/2	115	11.5	20	51	37	94		

KNITTING NEEDLES CONVERSION CHART

Canada/U.S.	0	1	2	3	4	5	6	7	8	9	10	10½	11	13	15
Metric (mm)	2	2¼	2¾	3¼	3½	3¾	4	4½	5	5½	6	6½	8	9	10

CROCHET HOOKS CONVERSION CHART

Canada/U.S.	1/B	2/C	3/D	4/E	5/F	6/G	8/H	9/I	10/J	10½/K	N
Metric (mm)	2.25	2.75	3.25	3.5	3.75	4.25	5	5.5	6	6.5	9.0

Annie's® A Granny Square Christmas is published by Annie's, 306 East Parr Road, Berne, IN 46711. Printed in USA. Copyright © 2016, 2018 Annie's. All rights reserved. This publication may not be reproduced in part or in whole without written permission from the publisher.

RETAIL STORES: If you would like to carry this publication or any other Annie's publication, visit AnniesWSL.com.

Every effort has been made to ensure that the instructions in this publication are complete and accurate. We cannot, however, take responsibility for human error, typographical mistakes or variations in individual work. Please visit AnniesCustomerService.com to check for pattern updates.

ISBN: 978-1-59012-573-1